The PAINTER & MOTHER

Eva Howarth

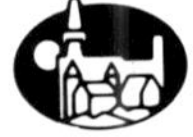

Salem House Publishers
Topsfield, Massachusetts

Created and produced by
PHOEBE PHILLIPS EDITIONS

First published in the United States
by Salem House Publishers, 1989,
462 Boston Street, Topsfield, Massachusetts 01983

ISBN 0 88162 458 6

Design: Caroline Reeves
Typeset by J&L Composition Ltd
Colour origination by Columbia Offset
Printed in Italy by Rotolito Lombarda

Introduction to
The PAINTER and The MOTHER

The centre of our lives in childhood and a beloved image forever – 22 artists, including Correggio, Chardin, Whistler and Picasso give substance to our ideals of maternal love and devotion spanning eight hundred years.

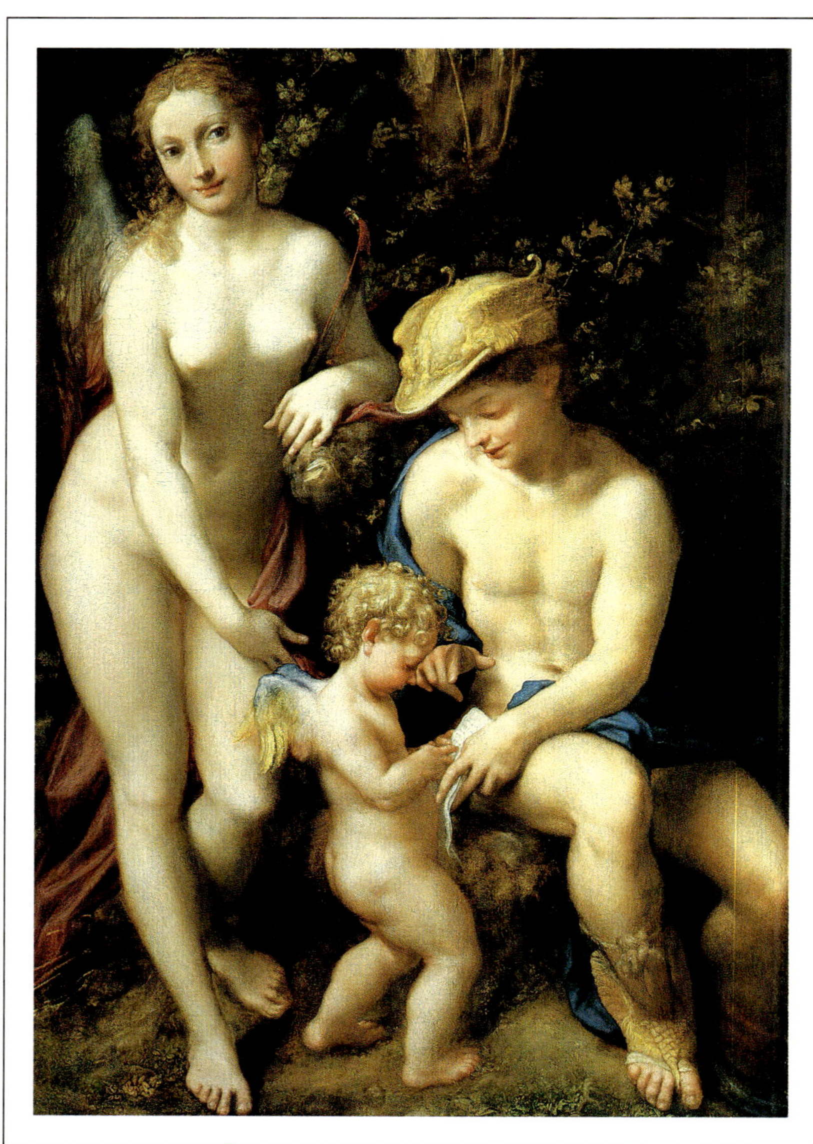

Mercury Instructing Cupid

Correggio (Antonio Allegri)

Italian c.1489–1534 National Gallery, London

The earliest celebrations of motherhood came to us long before Christian belief; ancient Greeks and Romans both worshipped a goddess of Beauty who was also the Mother of Love, and their stories have enlivened Western art ever since. The sixteenth-century preoccupation with pagan mythology was never more delightfully illustrated than in this picture; Cupid is watched with maternal pride by his mother, Venus, as he learns from Mercury.

Although Venus was married to Mars, a jealous husband and the God of War, she also had many lovers and Mercury, the fleet-footed Messenger of the Gods identified by his winged boots, was sometimes named as one of them.

The Renaissance court around Correggio was well-versed in all the classical legends and no doubt appreciated this particular glimpse of a somewhat unconventional 'family'. Such subjects gave artists the excuse for painting nude figures with strong erotic overtones which would otherwise be frowned on by the Church, still the main patron of most great artists.

Correggio took his name from the small Italian town where he was born. Acknowledged as one of the great masters of the Italian High Renaissance, he is known for his altarpieces and ceiling frescoes, but it was his magnificently sensuous painting of mythological subjects that earned him the nickname 'Painter of the Graces'.

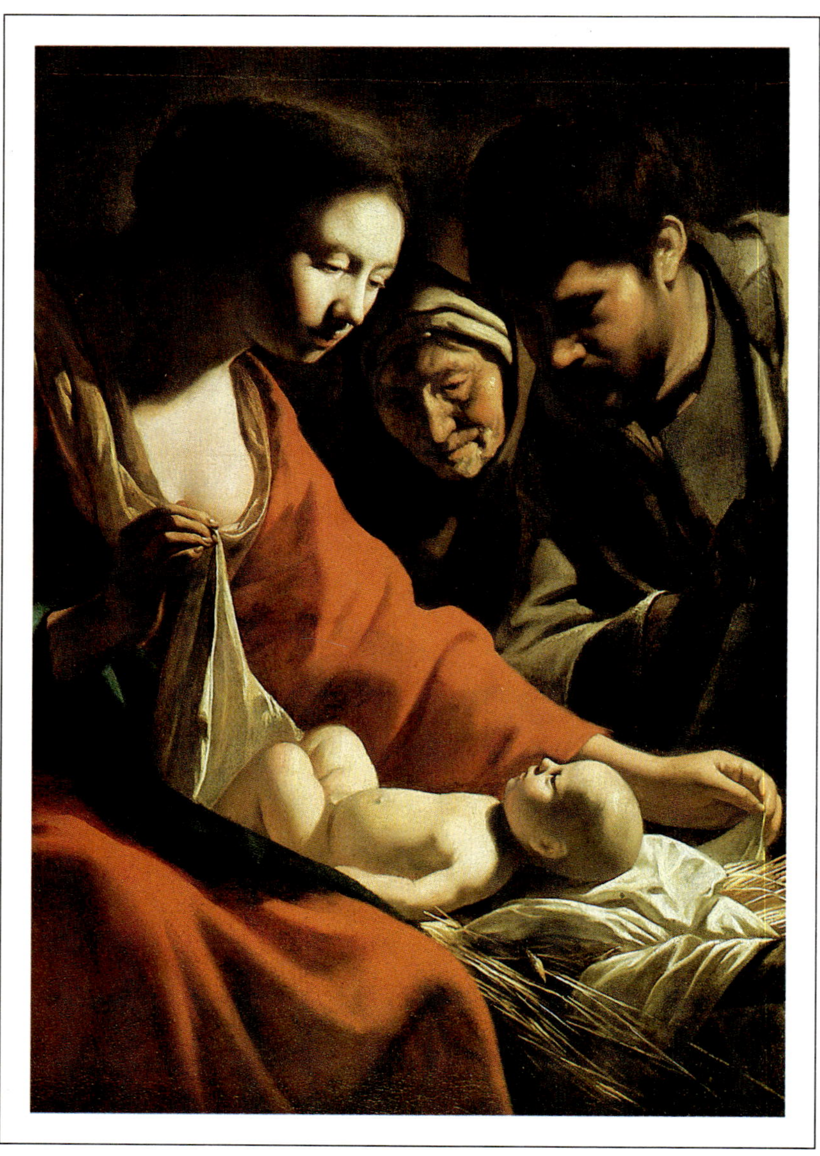

The Nativity

Louis Le Nain

French *c.* 1593–1648 Private Collection

In spite of popular pagan myths, traditional Christian beliefs in the essential purity of motherhood were central to Western Art during the long period of its development.

Medieval artists had usually shown both the Madonna and the Child as symbols but here the light from a torch reveals a very human Child, although the Madonna seems withdrawn into a world of her own, gazing at her child.

Le Nain's simple grouping is set off by the simple red dress, in complete contrast to the elaborate blue gowns of earlier Nativity paintings.

Louis Le Nain was the most talented of three brothers, all of whom were painters. As all three of them signed their paintings only as Le Nain, without any initials, historians have had to decide for themselves on purely stylistic grounds which brother painted which picture; in this serene study, they believe that the shepherds are portraits of all three Le Nains.

Louis is best known for his very realistic paintings of scenes from peasant life, and that is entirely born out by the composition and setting for the Holy Family; his style was a startling innovation in seventeenth-century France.

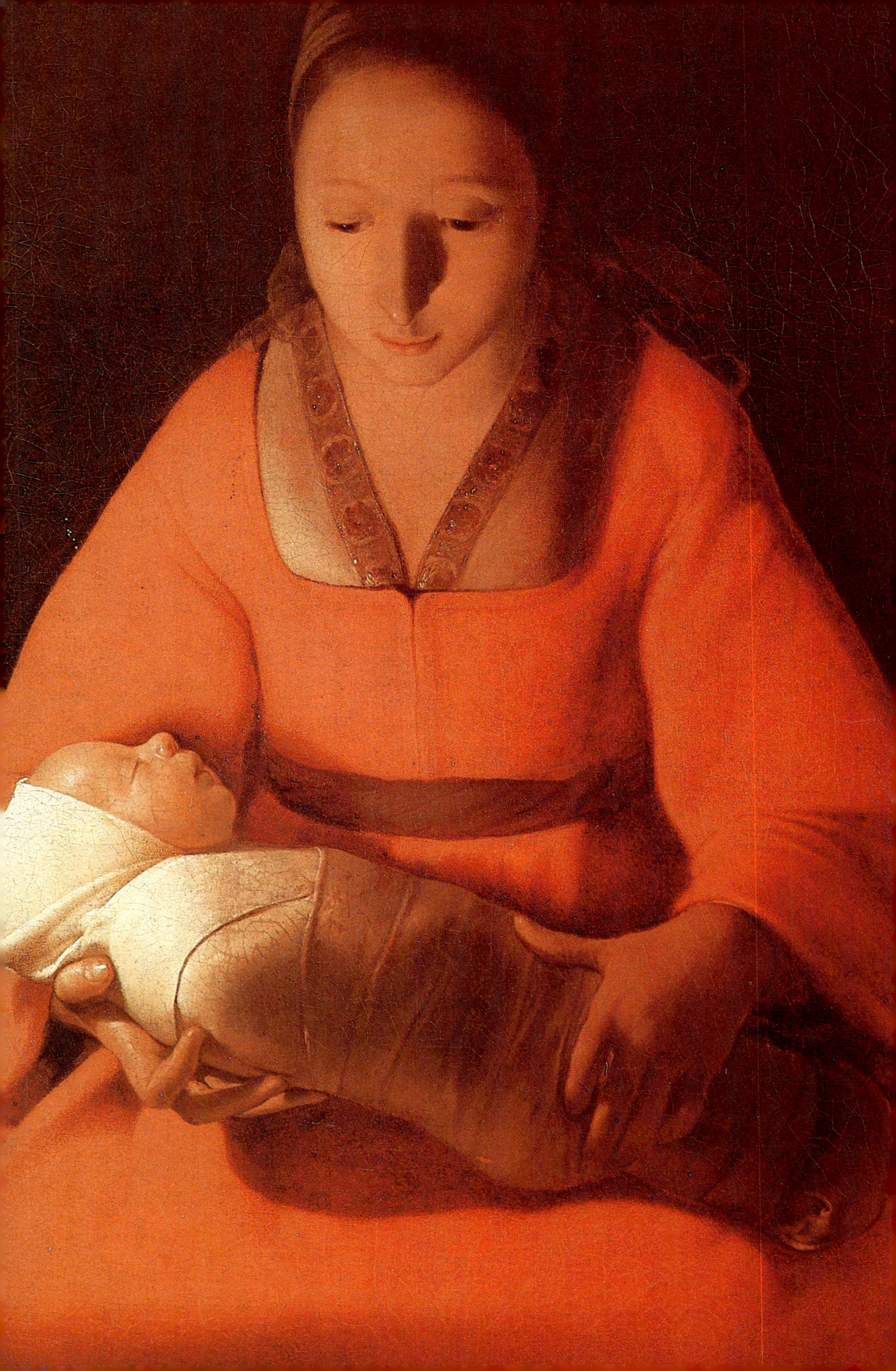

The Newborn Child

Georges de la Tour

French 1593–1652 Musée des Beaux-Arts, Rennes

A young mother sits perfectly still, hardly daring to breathe in case she wakes her newborn child. The stillness, the wonder, the unimaginable joy mixed with fear of the responsibility for another life when her own is only just beginning . . . the scene is apparently so tranquil, and yet so full of emotion that it seems possible that La Tour's models were his own wife and child.

Louis XIII hung one of La Tour's paintings in his bedchamber and was so impressed by it that he soon ordered all the other paintings in the room to be removed. Yet in spite of his royal patron, and considerable success during his life-time, La Tour's work sank into oblivion for almost three hundred years. Today he is regarded as one of the great masters of candlelit scenes.

The recent discovery of the details of his life and of those few of his paintings that survive is an artistic detective story, and even today there are continual arguments over whether his best-known paintings are truly his or contemporary, even modern, fakes. The first chance the public had to see a collection of La Tour's paintings was in Paris in 1972.

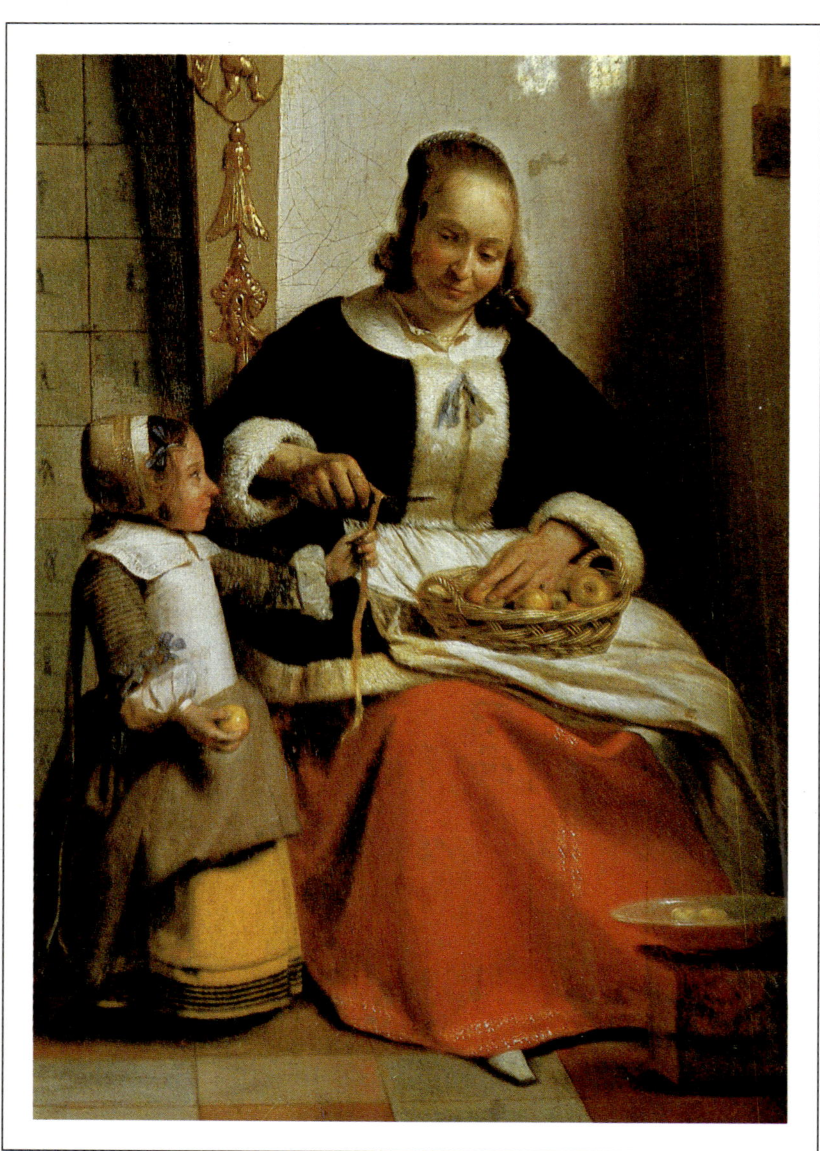

Interior with a Woman Peeling Apples

Pieter de Hooch

Dutch 1629–1684 Wallace Collection, London

These interior scenes, one of the glories of Dutch painting, celebrate an entirely new kind of art, with portraits of ordinary people rather than religious symbols or mythical gods. The new, middle-class patrons of the artists wanted their own lives, their homes and their accomplishments on the walls for all to enjoy and admire.

Dutch wives and mothers were respected as down-to-earth, practical members of the household. Here, judging by her modest but elegant clothes, the woman might be the wife of a well-to-do merchant with a number of servants. However, in Holland, a good mother believed firmly in education by example, especially for little girls who were going to be running their own homes one day. It was the pride of every housewife that no matter what time an unexpected visitor might arrive the house would be spotlessly clean and tidy, with plenty of food in the larder for comfortably vast meals and at least one dish of cooked apples on the stove!

De Hooch, an acknowledged master of the use of indoor and outdoor light for special effects, was best-known for his indoor and courtyard scenes. Some were painted to commission, but these interior scenes were also painted on speculation, to catch the eye of a new patron on a visit to the studio. The same fireplace or detail of a bed may turn up in six or seven paintings, presumably modelled on the artist's own home.

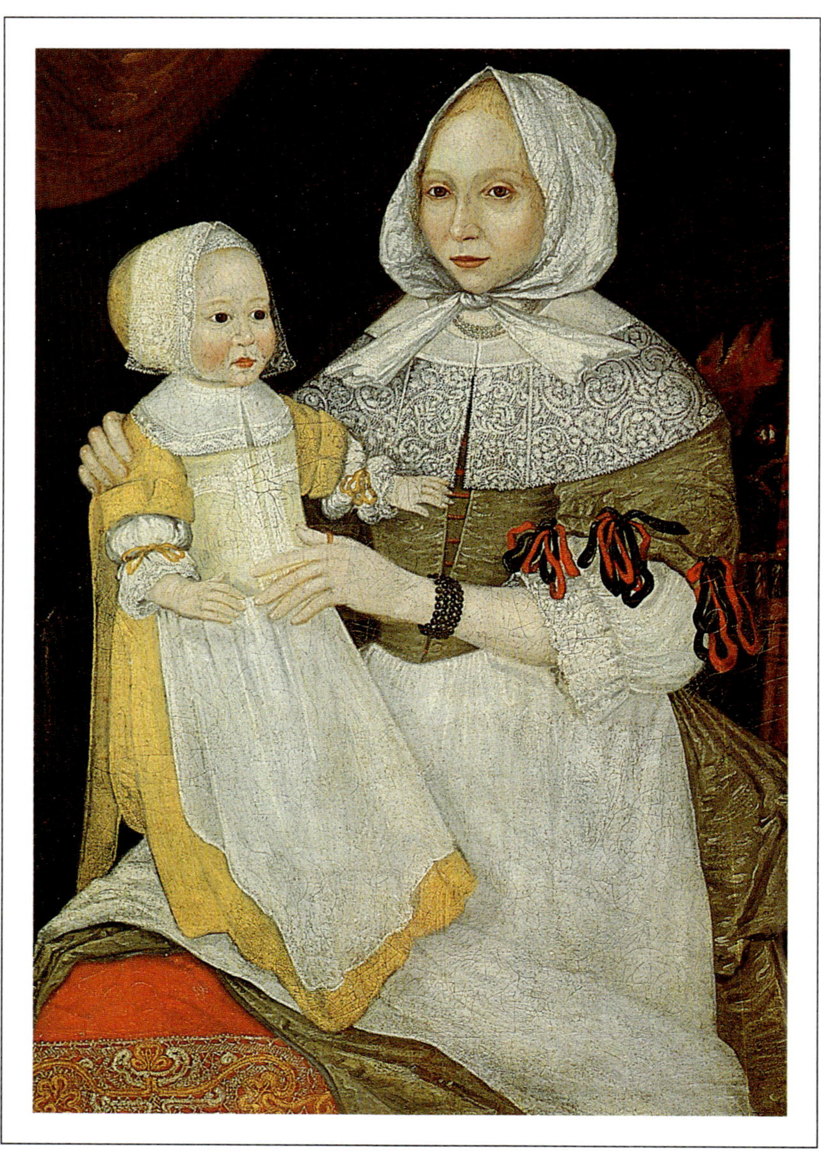

Mrs Freake and Baby Mary

Unknown Artist

American *c.* 1670 Worcester Art Museum, Massachusetts

Settlers in the new American colonies were anxious to have their families carefully represented in paintings to adorn the walls of their homes, just as their largely English and Dutch ancestors did. Mrs Freake has obviously put on one of her best dresses, with ribbons and a lace collar, but the American lifestyle is beginning to change some restrictive customs; baby Mary's clothes are far simpler and more practical than her English cousins' would have been. The anonymous artist has not been able to capture very much of a maternal relationship in the faces, but the mother's supporting hand is a lovely touch.

In the villages of New England it was difficult for talented young artists to learn their trade. Some became travelling painters, given commissions by the wealthier settlers, and they were often happy to paint store signs, inn boards, furniture, walls, boxes – in fact anything at all.

The Freake family commissioned a number of paintings in the 1670s and, although the poses are stiff and awkward, the detail is carefully recorded and the painting makes an immediate impression of a vigorous personality.

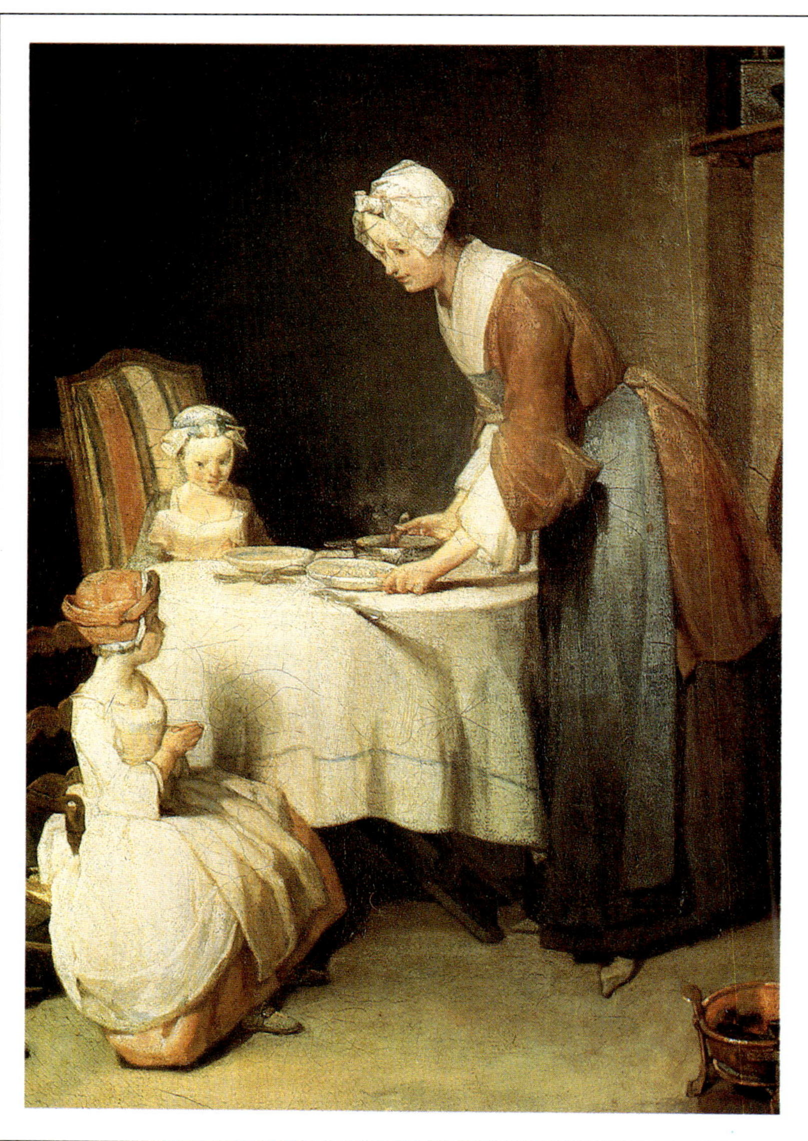

Saying Grace

Jean-Baptiste-Siméon Chardin

French 1699–1779 Louvre, Paris

The mother is just starting to serve the meal. She stops to help her little son with the next words in the prayer, while his sister seems to be enjoying her brother's difficulties. In the eighteenth century very young boys were dressed in skirts, but the drum hanging on the chair tells us that this is a little boy rather than a girl.

By this time, the Dutch fashion for scenes of everyday middle-class life had spread throughout the rest of Europe, with the mother as the active and central figure of the household. She was now the source of religious education as well as of comfort, food, and nursing care – an image which largely still exists. This scene could have been painted at any time, from seventeenth-century Holland to twentieth-century America, where Norman Rockwell's cover illustrations for *Saturday Evening Post* drew on similar themes.

Chardin was famous for his still-lifes and scenes from bourgeois households. The people in his paintings are, with few exceptions, servant girls, governesses, visitors, bourgeois mothers and children and, occasionally, wealthier women.

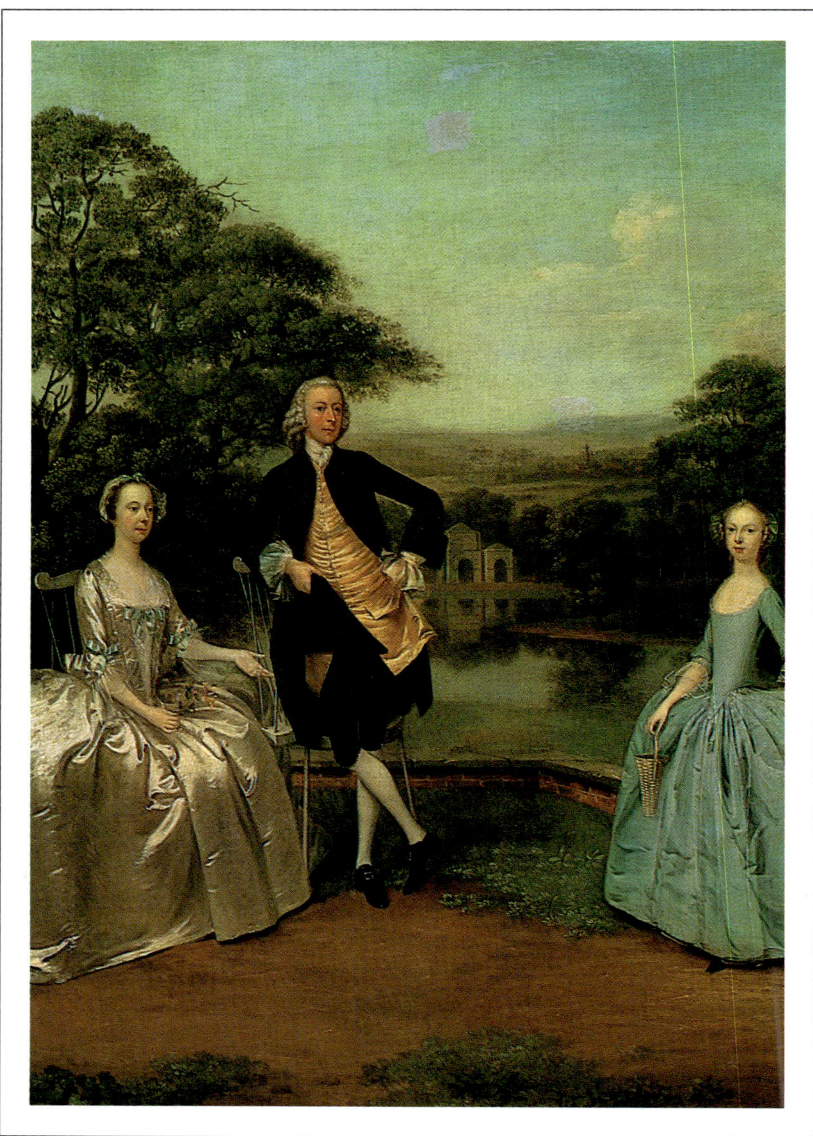

The James Family

Arthur Devis

English 1711–1787 Tate Gallery, London

From De Hooch's and Chardin's comfortable middle-class homes to the James's fashionable pretensions; there is no question of mother doing anything mundane like serving dinner or peeling apples; this is a display of wealth and taste rather than family life. Mrs James's gown probably came from Paris, then, as now, the fashion capital of Europe, and her two daughters, one of whom can be seen on the right, are suitably matched in simpler versions, although almost certainly made at home by a local dressmaker from a pattern book. The formal pose, the style of painting that the James chose, and our knowledge of English country life at the time would indicate that the children were brought up by nannies and governesses rather than their mother.

The artist was much concerned, too, that the painting showed off the rich silks and embroidered velvets his clients wore. Hoops – called 'panniers' after the French word for bread basket – were worn to extend skirts sideways; in extreme cases, as much as twelve feet across. It was impossible for two fashionably dressed ladies to sit side by side, let alone hold children on their laps. Even walking through doorways became a problem and curving, open staircases, easy to manoeuvre upon, became popular.

Devis is best-known for his portrait groups, his sitters being mainly rich merchants and country squires who liked to be painted with their families. His pictures tend to be rather formal, with the close attention to costumes seen here a typical feature.

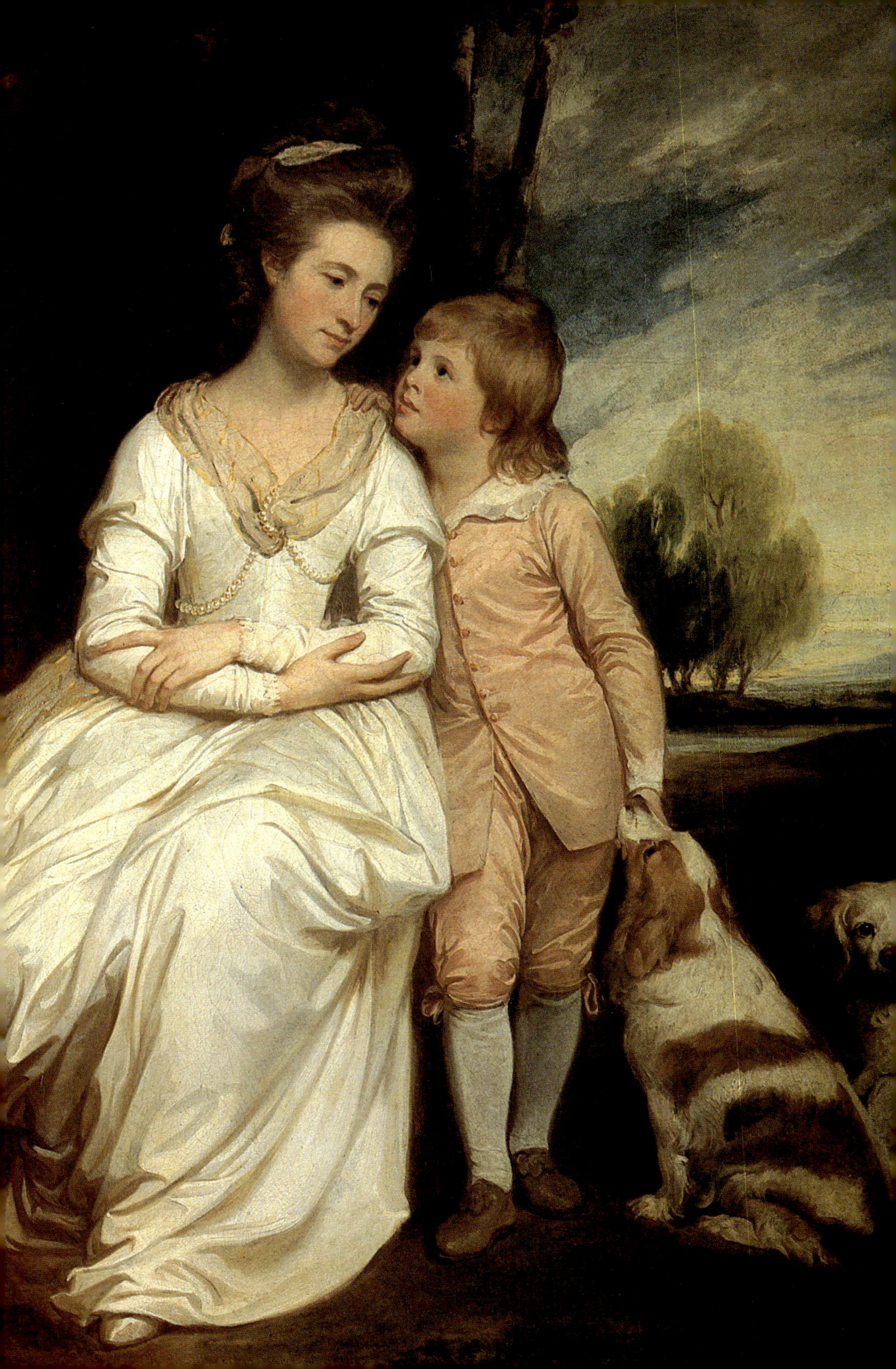

The Countess of Albemarle

George Romney

English 1734–1802 Kenwood House, London

Wealthy women in the eighteenth century had nurses, tutors or governesses to bring up their children, who usually lived on the nursery floor of the house, a long way from the rich and elegant rooms the adults used. When they did meet, usually for an hour or so at tea-time, the children were expected to be on their very best behaviour. They were taught to bow or curtsey to their mother, address her as 'Mama' or 'Madam', and never interrupt her busy life.

Yet, in spite of that, a few mothers and children succeeded in establishing a strong bond of mutual affection and in Romney's portrait the Countess seems to have achieved that sort of relationship with her elder son. There is a glimpse of warmth and mutual regard which makes a pleasant contrast to most society portraits of the time, where the children seem to be used as props in the picture to show off Mama's contribution to the family line.

Romney himself had been brought up in a much less privileged position; in his youth he travelled through the north of England in search of commissions. His usual price was two guineas and by the age of twenty-seven he had managed to save up a hundred pounds, part of which he gave to his wife, departing to London with the remainder.

There he became a successful historical and society portrait painter, best known to the public for his numerous portraits of Lady Hamilton.

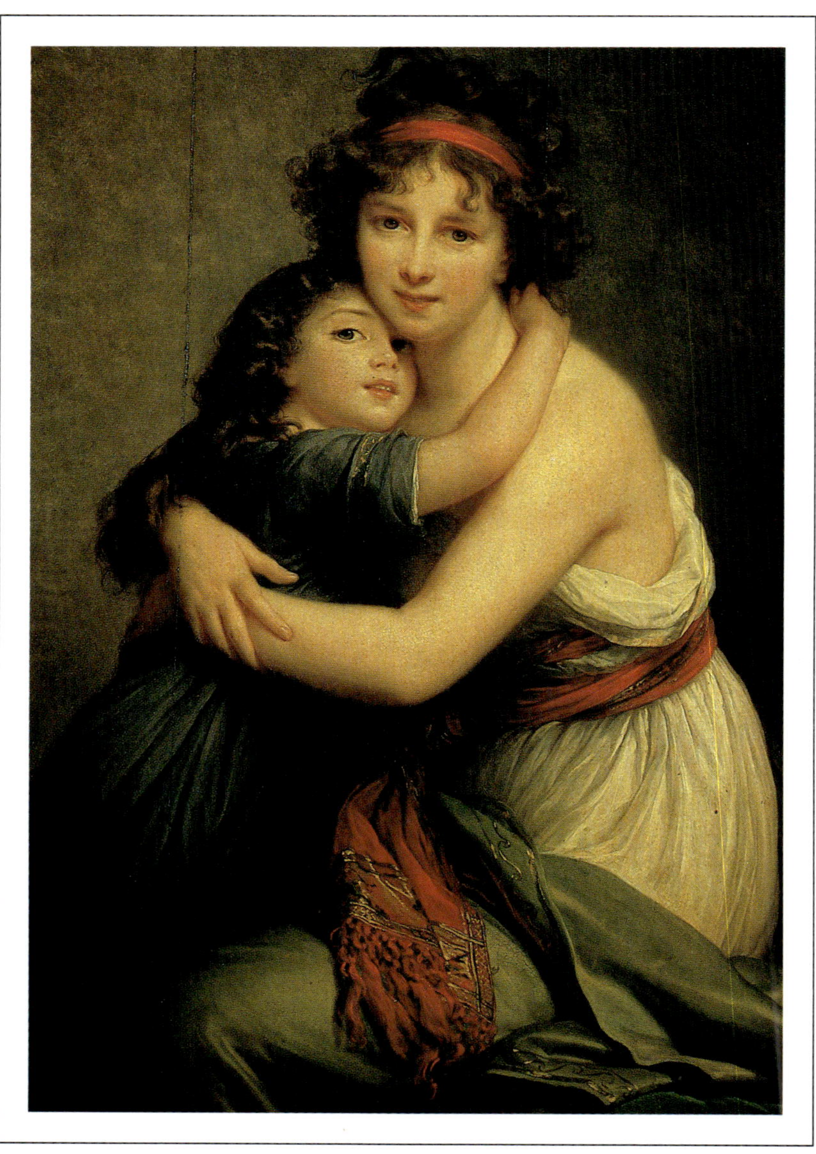

Mme Lebrun and Child

Élisabeth Vigée-Lebrun

French 1755–1842 Louvre, Paris

There are surprisingly few artists' paintings of themselves with their children, and because even fewer pre-twentieth-century portrait painters were women, almost none at all where the painter is both mother and subject. So here is a rare example indeed, and the result is delightful in concept, satisfying as a painting, and heart-warming as a subject, showing that a child's affection for its mother can withstand even the most formal bounds of eighteenth-century society.

Élisabeth Vigée-Lebrun started to paint at the age of fifteen. She was still very young when her father died and she supported her mother and herself by making copies of famous paintings, which were eagerly bought by the public. Her work was so admired, and her rise to fame so meteoric, that she was only twenty-seven years old when she painted the first of her many portraits of Queen Marie-Antoinette.

When the French Revolution broke out Mme Vigée-Lebrun left France and travelled extensively throughout Europe, receiving commissions to paint many famous people, among them Lady Hamilton, Madame de Stael, and several members of royalty. After the Revolution she returned to Paris, where her salon became the meeting place of well-known artists.

Yet still her most popular painting is this self-portrait. She was by all accounts a woman of great charm and beauty, which no doubt forms part of its appeal, but the work also conveys a mother's complete enchantment with her daughter, probably the reason for its great success.

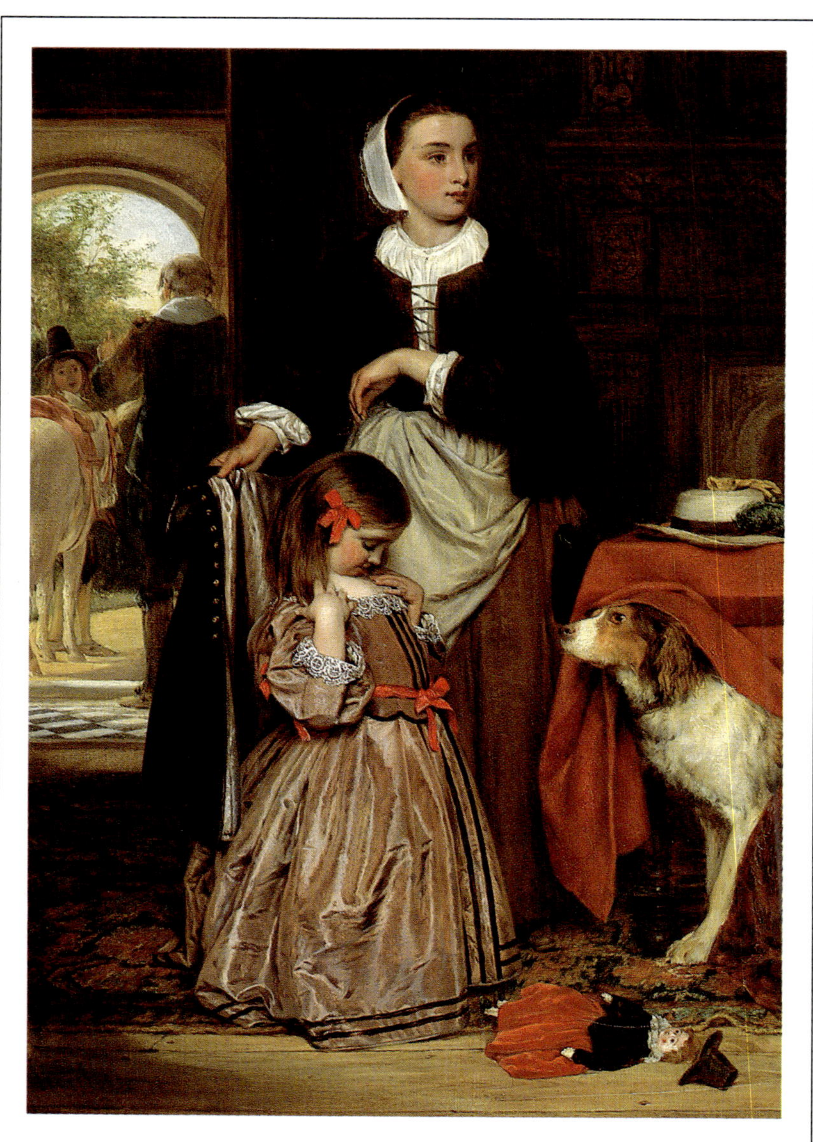

The New Dress

John Callcott Horsley

English 1817–1903 Private Collection

The little girl is clearly delighted with her new silk dress and the scene is made even more enjoyable by the attentive dog gazing adoringly at his small companion. The far-away look on her mother's face might be caused by the cost of the soon-to-be outgrown outfit, complete with velvet satin-lined coat.

The Victorian revival of Dutch family scenes was probably encouraged by the matriarchal influence of the English Queen, and her insistence that children should be an integral part of everyday life, whether in her own palace or in a simpler country home, like the one represented here. One small anachronism gives the painter away – in an original seventeenth-century Dutch painting, the oriental rug would probably have been on the table, rather than on the floor.

Horsley first made his name as a painter of historical subjects; he was also a musician, a friend of Mendelssohn and a regular contributor of drawings to Punch. Later he began to specialize in contemporary scenes variously described as 'sunshine and pretty women' and 'flirtation in the countryside'.

It was all very decorously done. Indeed, when he became Rector of the Royal Academy in his late fifties, he caused some trouble by his objections to nude models. As a result he became popularly known as Clothes-Horsley.

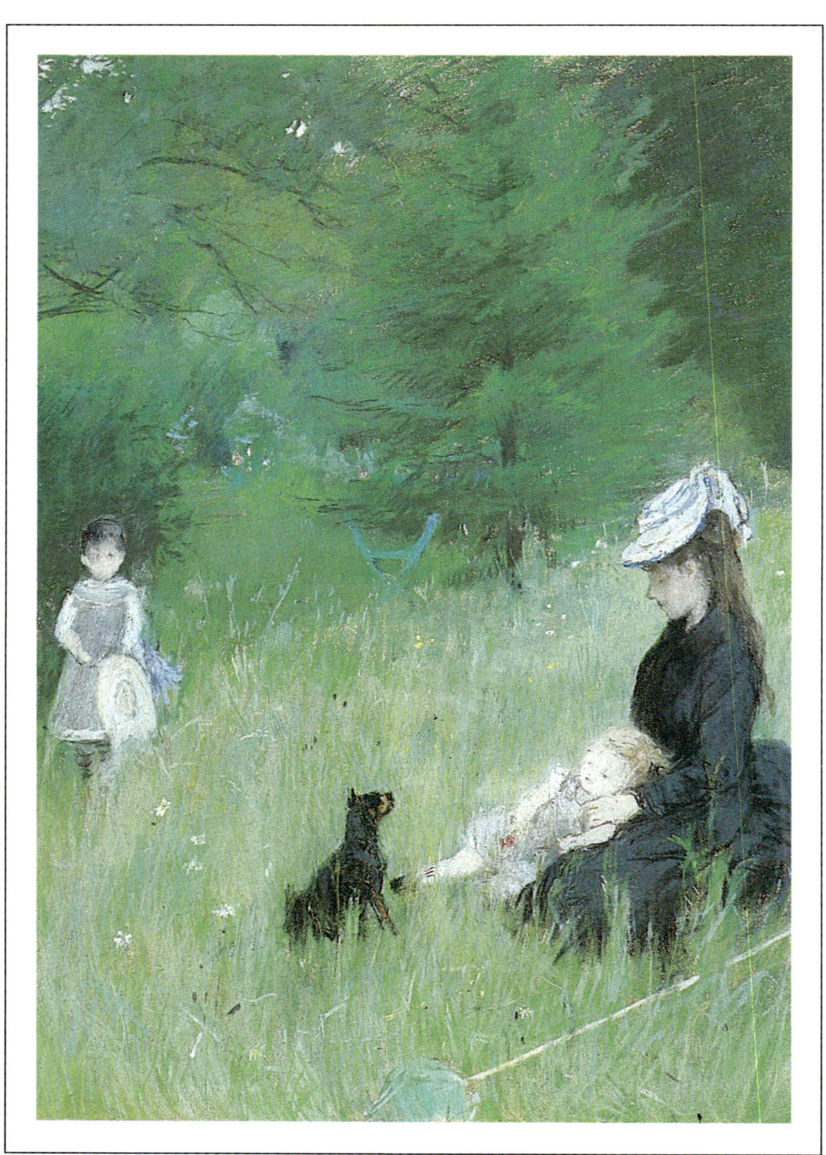

In the Park

Berthe Morisot

French 1841–1895 Museum de Petit Palais, Paris

Madame Morisot was a very attractive woman whose paintings reflect much of her own charm and femininity. Many of her paintings show one of her favourite models, her own daughter Julie, whose life she recorded from the cradle to young womanhood. Frequently there are two children in the picture; the second girl is usually Jeannie Gobillard, her niece and Julie's playmate.

Berthe Morisot came from a well-to-do family; her father was a patron of the arts and encouraged his daughter in her ambition to be a painter. She was fortunate in becoming the pupil and life-long friend of Edouard Manet, whose brother she eventually married.

The park in the picture is probably the Bois-de-Boulogne in Paris, not very far from the artist's studio. As a member of the Impressionist circle her paintings were regularly exhibited at the Paris Salon and at other venues, but her reputation grew posthumously until today her paintings are highly regarded as a true reflection of her time.

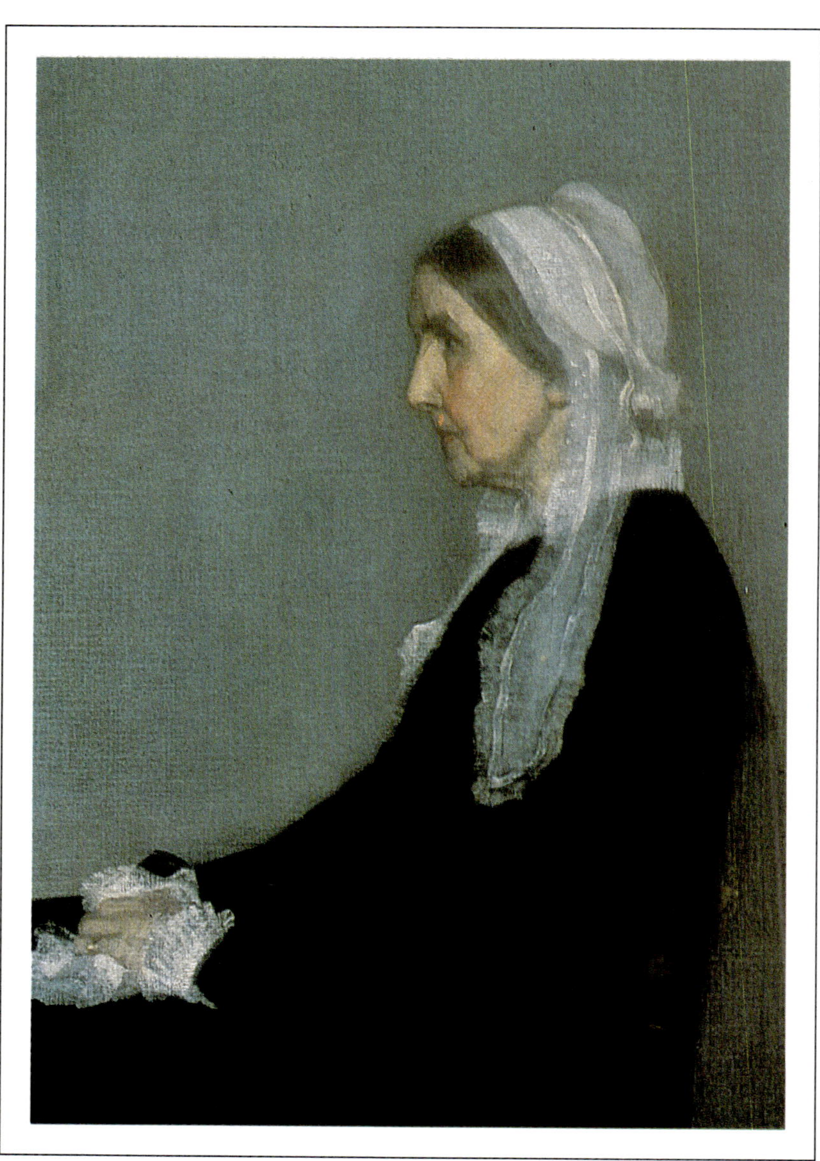

The Artist's Mother

James Abbott McNeill Whistler

American 1834–1903 Louvre, Paris

To the general public this is probably one of the most famous pictures of all, and certainly the one that springs to mind immediately on the subject of artists and motherhood. It is a long way from the pastel happiness of Impressionist children with their pretty mothers; it has beauty rather than prettiness, with an atmosphere of serenity, dignity, and a certain withdrawal from emotional ties; this is a record of a life coming to a close.

This portrait of Mrs George Washington Whistler, known always as Whistler's Mother, is signed with a butterfly, his usual signature. The painting was bought by the city of Paris in 1891.

James McNeill Whistler was born in the United States, but during part of his boyhood he lived at the Russian Court, where his father was working for the Tsar. After a number of years studying in Paris he came to England, where he spent most of his working life.

He became a very successful painter but was not personally the most popular of men; he once lost all his money when he brought an action for libel against an offensive art critic.

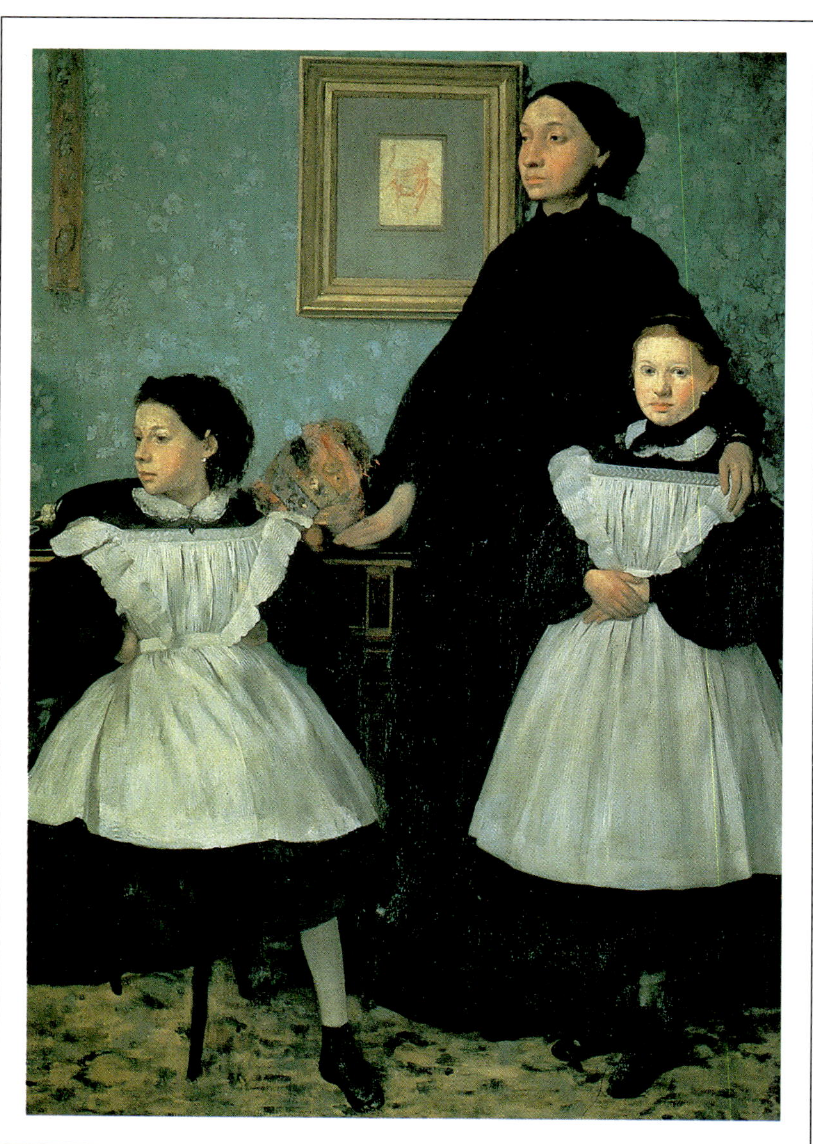

The Bellelli Family

Edgar Degas

French 1834–1917 Louvre, Paris

The mother of the two little girls is the Baroness Bellelli, Degas's aunt. The severity of the striking black and white composition is softened by the patterned carpet, wallpaper and, most clearly, the picture on the wall. One feels that Degas was more interested in the composition than the sitters; perhaps at the time two little girls weren't as exciting a project as the ballet dancers or circus performers which he admired and painted so often.

Strangely enough, unlike other Impressionists, Edgar Degas never painted from nature. He would work from notes, sketches and a large number of drawings, but would always paint the final picture in his studio.

Degas hated to part with his paintings. After his death four important sales were held in Paris to dispose of the hundreds of works which were found in his studio.

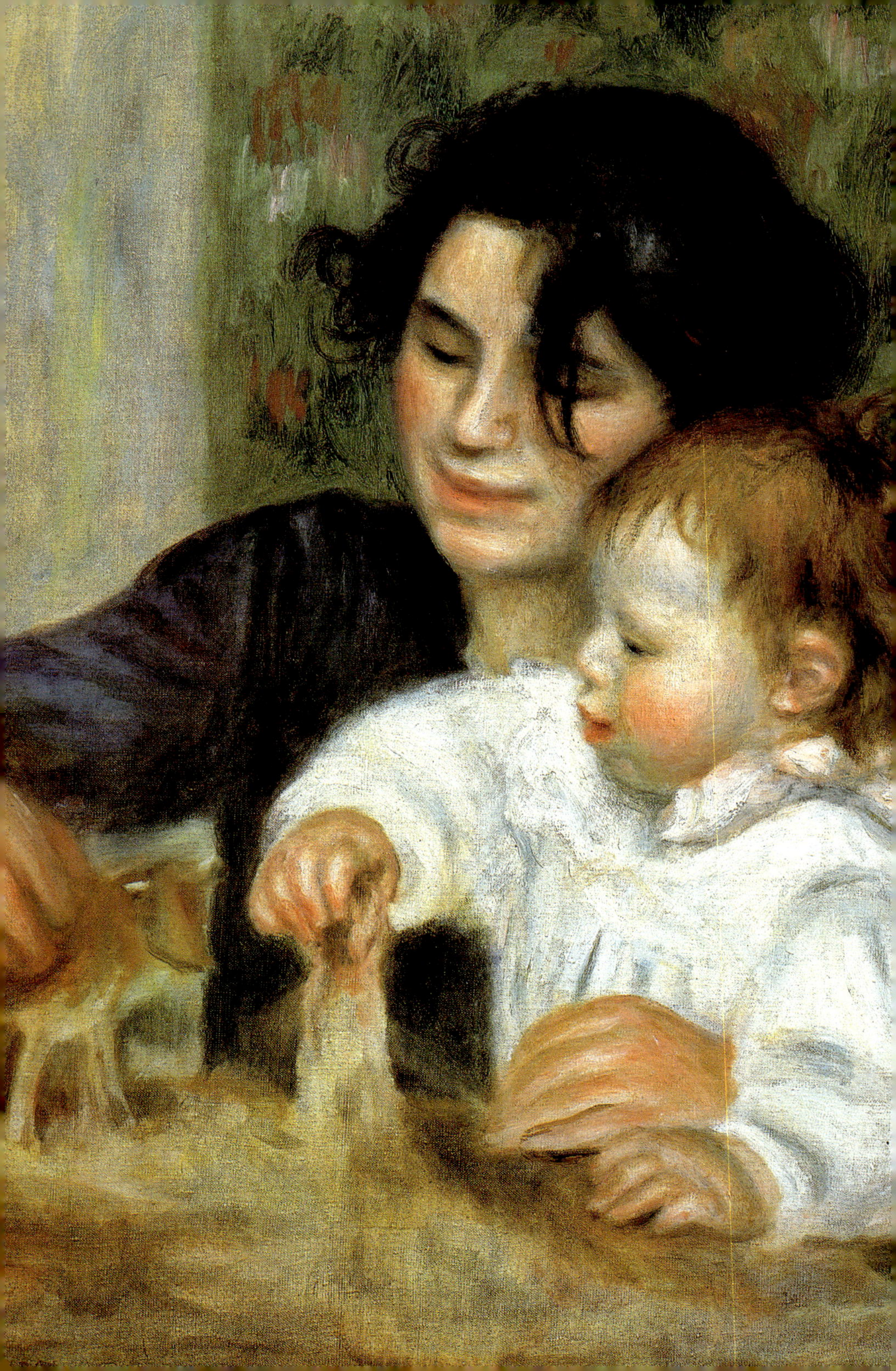

Gabrielle and her Children

Pierre-Auguste Renoir

French 1841–1919 Musée d'Orsay, Paris

There is no doubt that Renoir loved painting the female sex from small, wide-eyed babies to richly sensual women at moments of quiet intimacy, in the bath, sitting in the garden, playing with their children. Gabrielle, a simple peasant girl with the sturdy body and round face that Renoir adored, lived originally as a servant with Madame and Monsieur Renoir and their three children, but she also became Renoir's model and had children by him. Their extended family was celebrated by the artist in many portraits and drawings, and the deep affection he felt for them shows clearly in the rounded composition, the warm colours and the physical closeness of the three bodies in this painting.

By this time the work of the Impressionists had begun to make art critics and the general public revise their earlier opinions. In their early days nearly all the group had had a hard struggle and few dealers were willing to buy their work. Paintings which today sell for a fortune sold originally for the price of a canvas or a dinner – but gradually Impressionism became admired and Renoir was among those who became famous and successful.

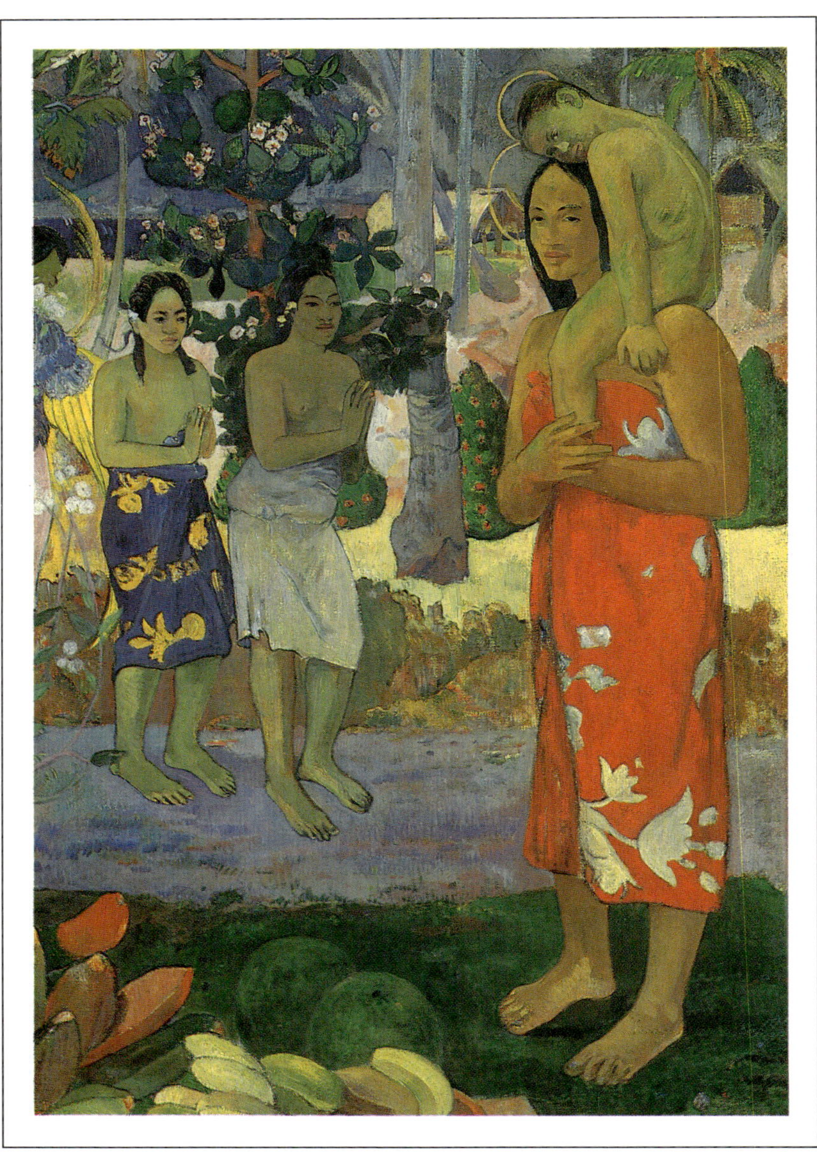

Orana Maria

Paul Gauguin

French 1848–1903 Metropolitan Museum of Art, New York

The Tahitian title of the painting can be translated as 'We Greet Thee, Mary'. Gauguin shows Mary and the Child as he thought the islanders would visualize them, choosing for his models a Tahitian woman and her son, dressed in native fashion. In the background flowering trees form a typical local scene. The painting conveys too the easy-going and fundamentally happy life of Tahitian women. Naturally enough, this was seen as appalling blasphemy by the conventional Christian world, and Gauguin's reputation suffered from the resentment and even hysteria that his work inspired in Europe, where depicting the Madonna as a native woman was seen as degrading the reverence shown to her.

Paul Gauguin was a successful stockbroker before he became a painter. At the age of forty-three he decided to turn his back on civilization and went to live on the idyllic island of Tahiti. In his book *Noa Noa*, he wrote: 'I have escaped everything that is artificial and conventional. Here I enter into truth, become one with nature'. In spite of poverty and continual illness he painted his greatest pictures during this period.

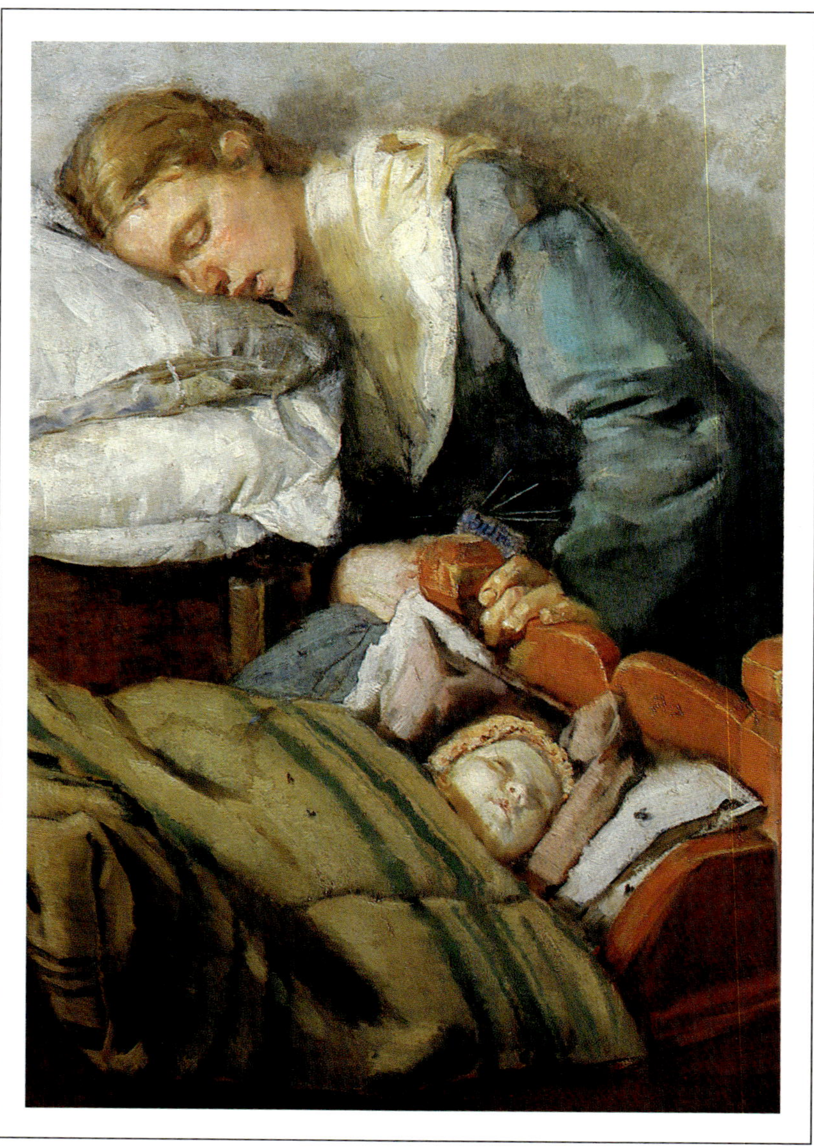

Sleeping Mother

Christian Krohg

Norwegian 1852–1925 Private Collection

The mother is clearly exhausted by the day spent with a demanding child, and she is painted sleeping profoundly alongside her baby. This is a tender study of a moment which must strike a chord of sympathy in most mothers struggling to bring up their children in a simple household. There is quiet reality in every corner of the room, not the immaculate household of the Dutch sixteenth century, but a modern nursery, with its brightly-painted, comfortable, even shabby furniture.

Christian Krohg specialized in depicting domestic and country scenes, and this is his most popular painting.

The theme of mother and child is a common one in art, from the religious adoration of medieval Madonnas to the gentle humanity of this century. Yet it was not until the twentieth century that in America a special day in the year was chosen for honouring 'motherhood' – a time to say thank you to the unsung heroines of the nursery. The idea was put forward by Anna Jarvis, who lived in Philadelphia, in 1907. Four years later Mother's Day was celebrated in every state, and the custom has now spread to other countries in Europe, Latin America, Africa and even in the Far East.

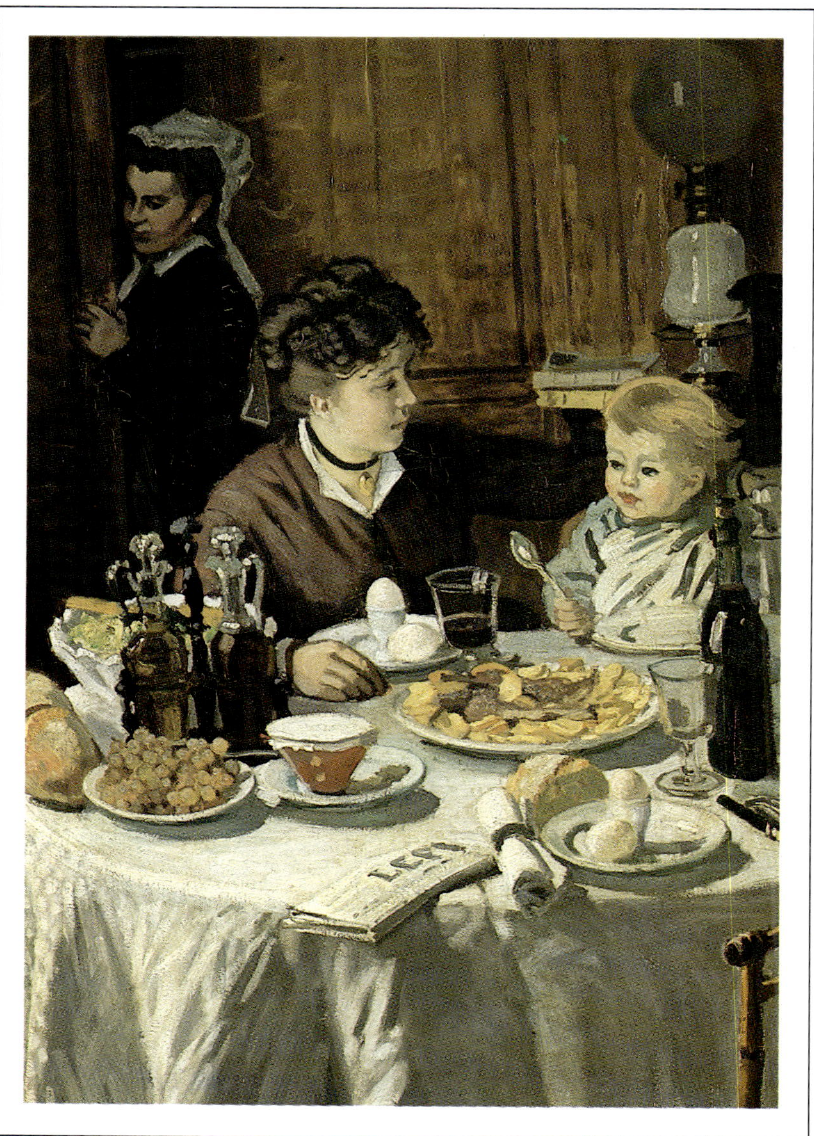

The Lunch

Claude Monet

French 1840–1926 Frankfurt Kunstinstitut, Frankfurt

The scene is a typical French middle-class dining room. The maid has set the table, and mother and son are sitting waiting for father to appear. His napkin is neatly folded and so is his newspaper. The wine is placed next to his glass. In short, everything is ready for father to enjoy his lunch; here is a painting which shows clearly that even at the beginning of the century, the world of women and children was incomplete until the centre of the household – and the only figure missing from the painting – appeared. Yet it was all done with affection and with supremely French style; the more so since it is possible that this was Monet's own family.

The word 'Impressionism' originated from a painting of Claude Monet's, called *Impression, Rising Sun*, which was first exhibited in 1874. An art critic coined the word with the intention of ridiculing the group of artists who painted in the new style.

Monet's work consisted largely of landscapes and a few still-lifes which showed a masterly presentation of atmosphere and colour. However, at the beginning of his career art dealers were still reluctant to buy from him and so he painted more conventional pictures, such as *The Lunch*, which he hoped would amuse and attract the general public.

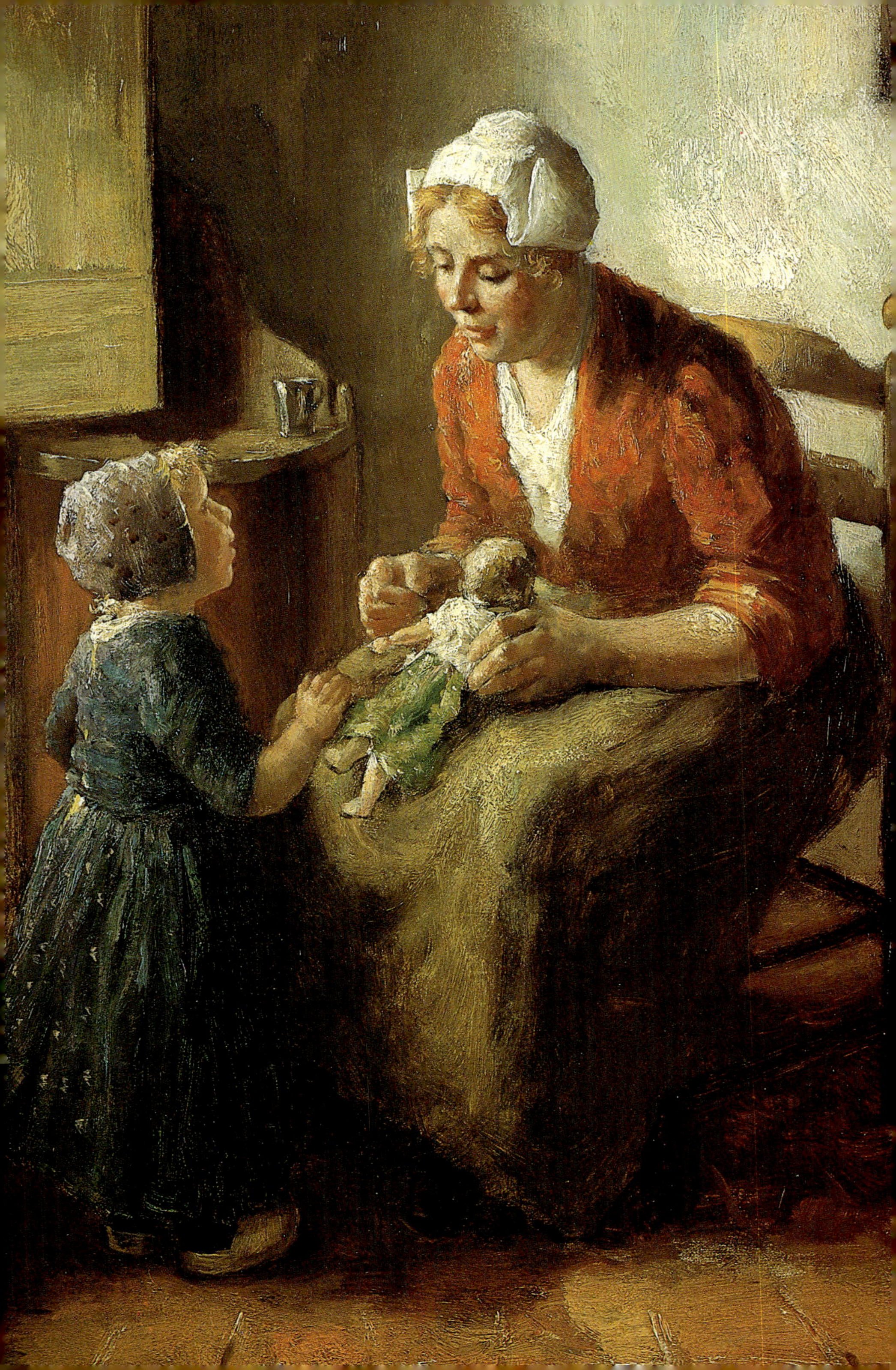

Mother and Child

Bernard de Hoogh

Dutch 1867–1943 Private Collection

The girl in the picture no doubt sees the doll as her own child with whom she must act the mother, as little girls have done through the ages. Baby dolls have been known since the earliest civilizations, and in many cultures dolls symbolize childhood itself – in Japan women wanting children have offered them at shrines, while child brides in India have commonly been presented with them.

The making of dolls and doll's houses has been a considerable industry in Europe for some three centuries. The products have become more and more sophisticated, and the modern child can buy for her doll a wonderful range of furniture, clothes and household equipment in miniature.

The finest dolls and doll's houses can be seen in museums. These are not just playthings but works of art in their own right, perfect miniatures which arouse delight and amazement at the way they reflect each century's fashions and customs.

Some of the finest dolls of all have been, and continue to be, produced in the Netherlands. Little is known about de Hoogh, a modern inheritor of the traditional Dutch fascination with household scenes, but he knew enough about children to give the girl's doll the importance it deserved.

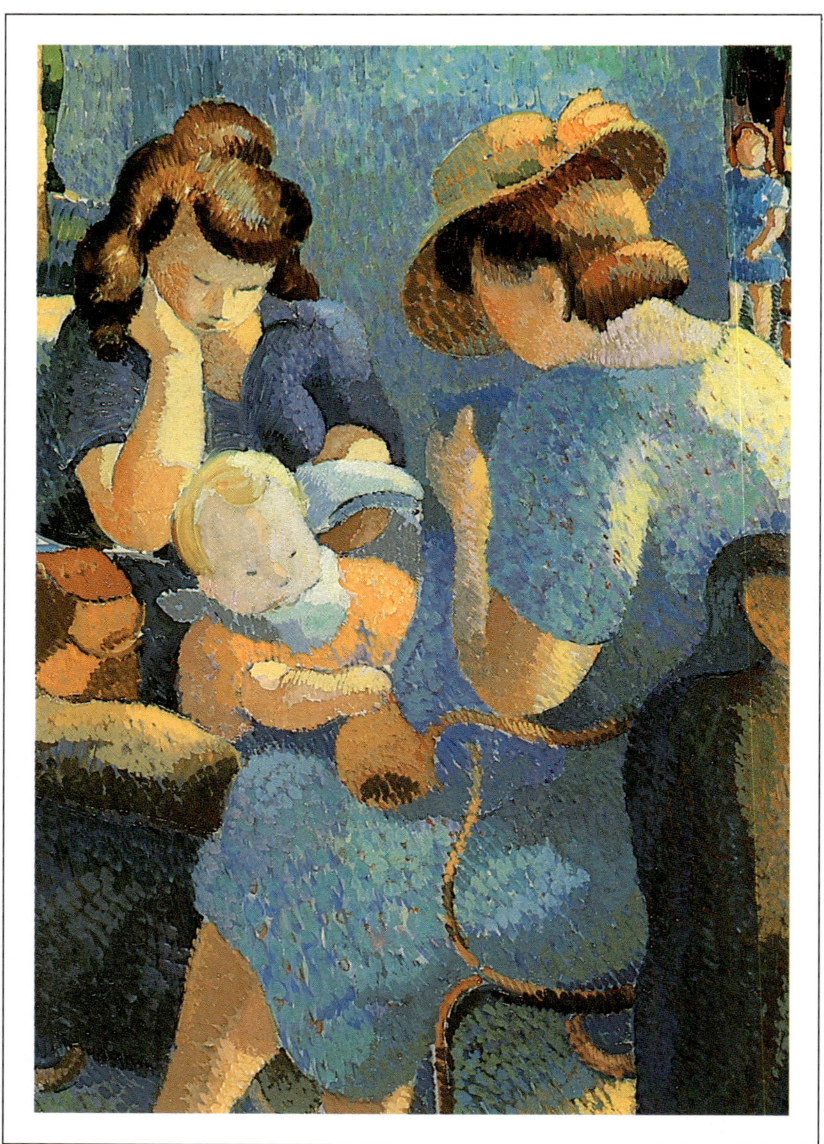

Luxembourg Gardens

Pierre de Belay

French 1890–1947 Musée des Beaux-Arts, Rouen

In every big city there are certain parks which attract mothers with young children. The Luxembourg Gardens, on the left bank of Paris, is one of these. There is even a puppet show there every afternoon and for older children there are statues representing all the queens of France as well as a group of figures of outstanding women from the nineteenth century.

Little is known about Pierre de Belay, but he was obviously influenced by the bright colours and simple shapes of the 1920s. The girls' clothes are smart and cheerful without being fussy, making areas of bright colour and giving an impression of a warm, sunny day in spring. These are comparatively modern mothers, taking care of their own children, enjoying time out for a little gossip and a drink of lemonade before going back to do the housework.

The history of the park goes back to the seventeenth century when Maria de' Medici, widow of Henry IV of France, built the Luxembourg Palace. The extensive green area around it, with its shady trees and wide gravel walks, was the meeting place of fashionable society. Today the palace is the seat of the Senate and the park is still a popular meeting place for university students, foreign visitors and, of course, mothers, who come from all over the city to spend the afternoon with their friends and their children.

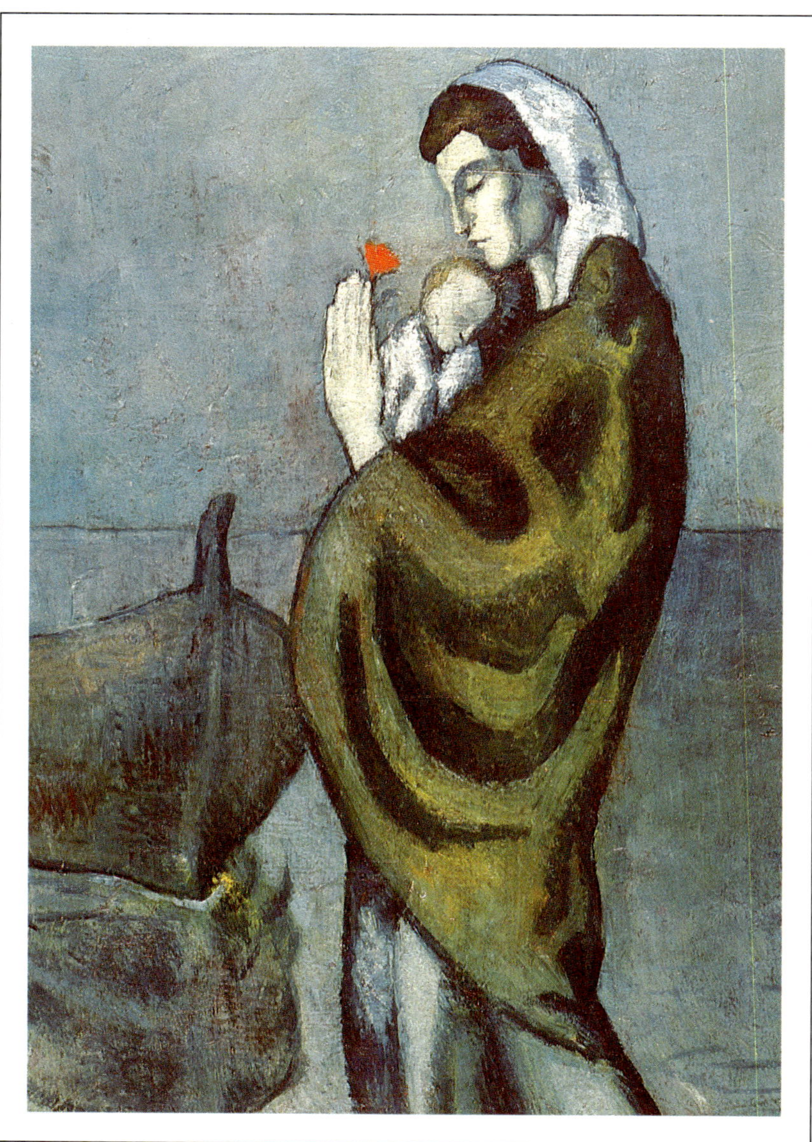

Mother and Child

Pablo Picasso

Spanish 1881–1973 Private Collection

Picasso is probably the best-known and certainly the most versatile artist of the twentieth century. During his long career he experimented with various new techniques and painted in a number of different styles.

Mother and Child was painted during his so-called 'blue period', which lasted from approximately 1901 to 1905. During most of this period Picasso was himself very poor and his paintings reflect a great understanding of, and compassion towards, human suffering, a subject to which he frequently returned in later life.

The woman in the painting could be any mother trying to remove her child from some disaster – war, famine or other calamity. The solitary figure standing against a vast sea conveys a tremendous sense of loneliness and despair.

The sombre mood of Picasso's paintings of this period is emphasized by the cold greenish-blue colour which dominates most of them. However, a sense of hope is conveyed by the single red flower in the mother's hand.

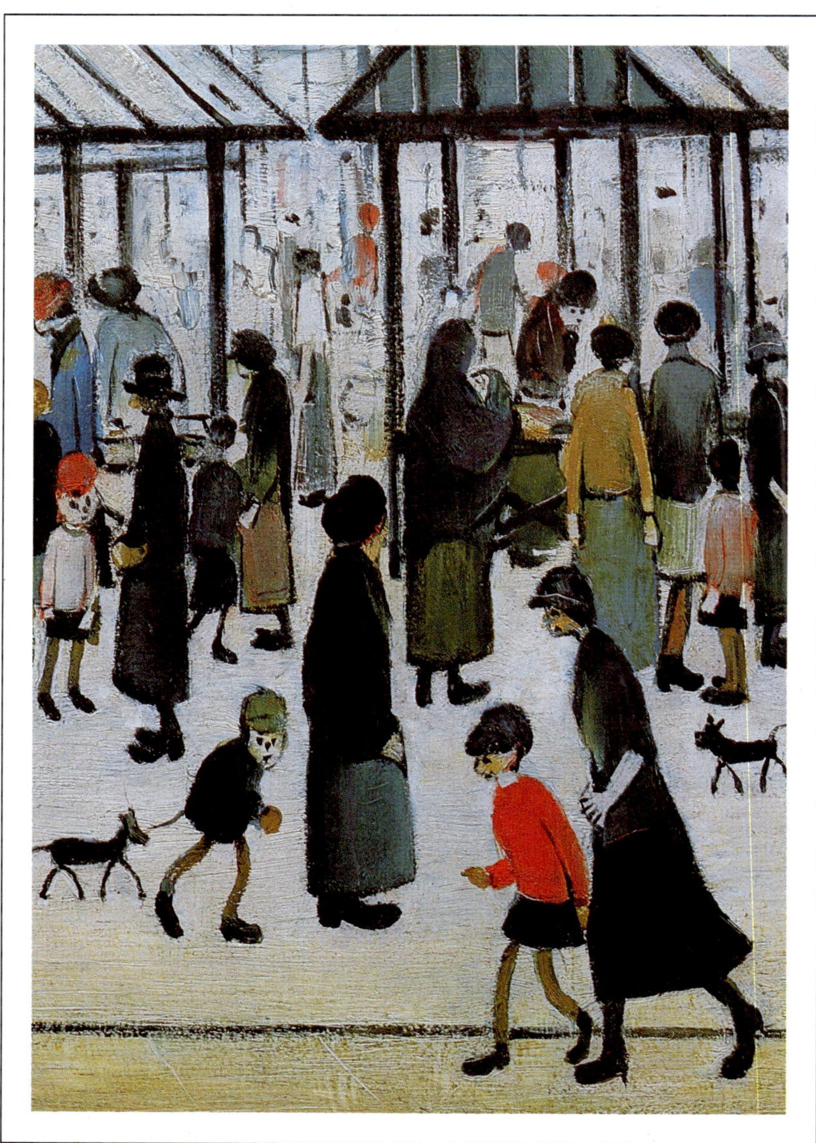

Market Scene

L. S. Lowry

English 1887–1976 — Salford Museum, Salford

In *Market Scene* mothers with their children are seen queueing, choosing, bargaining. In 1939, when this picture was painted, unemployment was high, especially in industrial cities, and women with large families often had a hard time making ends meet.

Lowry painted this world all his life, involving himself vicariously in the life of the town, with the people he saw on the street, creating little stories so you can see exactly who they are, where they are going, and even perhaps what they are going to do next! His colours are mainly subdued, and most of his pictures look as if they were seen through a thin layer of smog. But the figures are full of humour and individual character and gain emphasis from the plain white background, a characteristic feature of many of this artist's paintings.

Lowry lived most of his life in an industrial suburb of Manchester. He was in his early twenties when his family, because of financial problems, first moved there. His mother hated the place so much that for the next seven years until her death she refused to leave the house. Lowry, on the other hand, became fascinated by his environment. In his job as rent collector he could observe and record, although he always regarded his paintings as private scribbles, and it took a long time before his growing reputation as an artist made him famous.

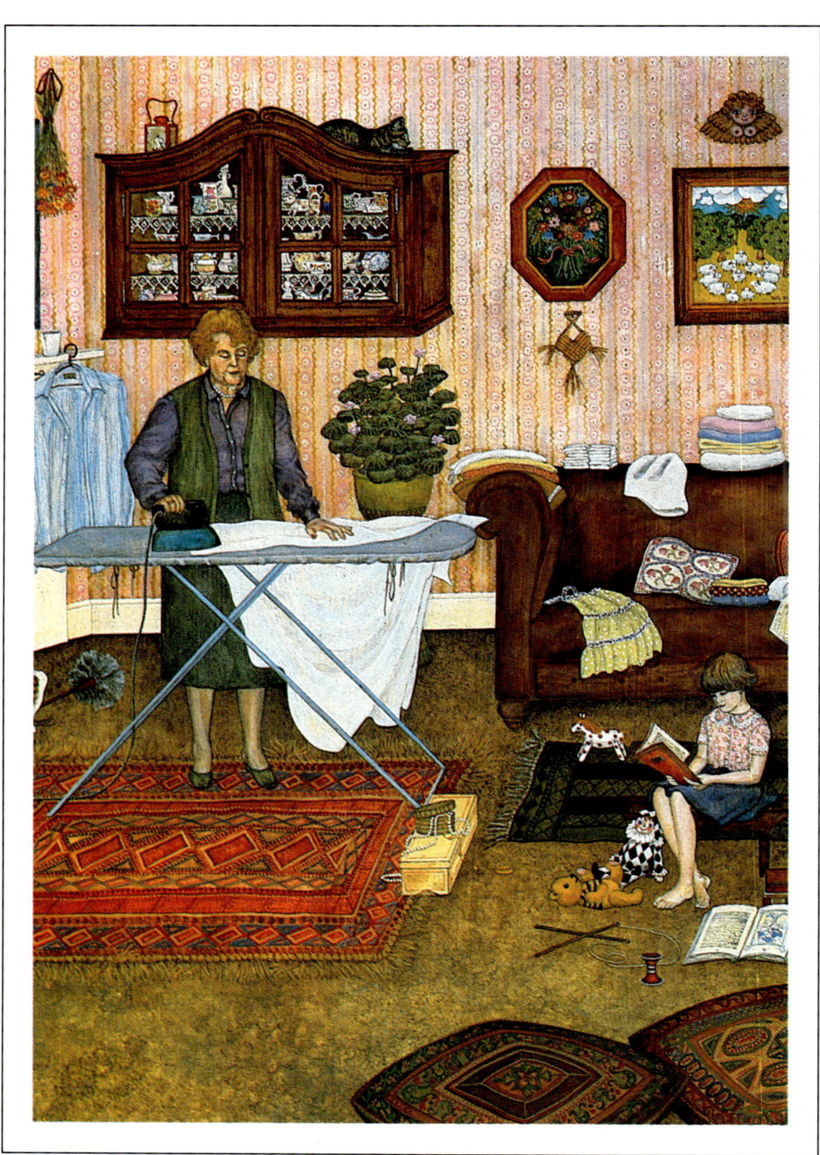

Ironing Day

Ditz (Dietlinde Nekuda)

Austrian living artist — Private Collection

The woman here is Ditz herself and the little girl is her daughter. This is another rare example of a female artist painting a self-portrait with child, but it is a very far cry from Madame Vigée-Lebrun's romantic image; this is modern reality. The setting is a spare room in the painter's house which is used for ironing, sewing and any other household chores.

The little girl is surrounded by books. It was an established custom in the family that whenever the artist had to do the ironing or sewing her daughter would come and read aloud to her.

On the floor, next to her toys and books, is a diabolo, an ancient children's game; on the wall is a picture of roses painted on glass with a corn dolly hanging beneath it, both of which are popular art forms in Austria. So the painting is a record of family history as well as a charming genre scene of modern life.

Dietlinde Nekuda was born in Vienna, married an Englishman and now lives in London. She signs all her paintings 'Ditz', an abbreviation of Dietlinde. *Ironing Day* was exhibited in the Royal Academy, London, in 1987.

Sources

CORREGGIO: *Mercury Instructing Cupid*
National Gallery, London

LE NAIN: *The Nativity*
Private Collection (Bridgeman)

DE LA TOUR: *The Newborn Child*
Musée des Beaux-Arts, Rennes (Bridgeman)

DE HOOCH: *Interior with a Woman Peeling Apples*
Wallace Collection, London

ANON: *Mrs Freake and Baby Mary*
Worcester Art Museum, Massachusetts

CHARDIN: *Saying Grace*
Louvre, Paris (Bridgeman)

DEVIS: *The James Family*
Tate Gallery, London

ROMNEY: *The Countess of Albemarle*
Kenwood House, London

LE BRUN: *Mme Le Brun and Child*
Louvre, Paris (Bridgeman)

HORSLEY: *The New Dress*
Private Collection (Bridgeman)

MORISOT: *In the Park*
Musée du Petit Palais, Paris (Bridgeman)

WHISTLER: *The Artist's Mother*
Louvre, Paris (Bridgeman)

DEGAS: *The Bellelli Family*
Louvre, Paris (Bridgeman)

RENOIR: *Gabrielle and her Children*
Musée d'Orsay, Paris (Bridgeman)

GAUGUIN: *Orana Maria*
Metropolitan Museum, New York

KROHG: *Sleeping Mother*
Billedgalleri, Bergen

MONET: *The Lunch*
Stüdelschische Kunstinstitut, Frankfurt

DE HOOGH: *Mother and Child*
Galerie George, London (Bridgeman)

DE BELAY: *Luxembourg Gardens*
Musée des Beaux-Arts, Rouen (Bridgeman)

PICASSO: *Mother and Child*
Christie's, London (Bridgeman)

LOWRY: *Market Scene*
Salford Art Gallery and Museum (Bridgeman)

DITZ: *Ironing Day*
Private Collection (Bridgeman)